TELL ME A STORY

TELL ME A STORY

Understanding Your Story in Light of Israel's Story

Doug Wadsworth

Bramblewood Press
Torrance, CA

ISBN-13: 978-0-9797665-9-6

Bramblewood Press
Torrance, CA

Printed in the United States of America

Contents

Foreword

At Friends Church our mission is to become a community of authentic Christ followers, compelled to change our world. This mission gets worked out as we gather together, grow together, and go together. In this study we will get to put some of that into practice. Over the next seven weeks you and your group will learn how God worked in the people of Israel, see how God has worked in your life, and begin to see how you fit into the incredible story of what God has done, is doing, and will do in the world.

As humans we are not meant to be alone, and while we can certainly grow by ourselves, our deepest and best growth comes when we grow with others. This is why community is so important to our church! Through this study with your group, you will have the opportunity to be the church in a smaller form, gathering together weekly to read and hear from God, growing together as you see how God has been at work, and going out together into the world.

Much like Rooted, we ask that each member of the group commit to holding the stories from the group in confidence. All that means is that we will hold each other's stories faithfully—we will not share without permission and we will not use a story improperly. We commit to carry each other's burdens, and to pray for each other, as well as to lovingly tell each other the truth.

We are excited to see what you learn, and how you grow as individuals and as a group!

Week 1

What's Your Story?

1 Peter 2:9-10. But you are a chosen people, a royal priest-hood, a holy nation, God's special possession, that you may declare the praises of him who called you out of darkness into his wonderful light. Once you were not a people, but now you are the people of God; once you had not received mercy, but now you have received mercy. (NIV)

Who are you? This is one of the first questions that we ask when we meet someone new. It is a question that can be answered in myriad different ways. If you ask me, I can tell you that I am Doug Wadsworth. I am Veronica's husband, Sofia, Amy, and Charles' dad, and Mark and Carolyn's son. I can tell you that I work as a computer programmer, and I have just completed my Master's of Divinity degree. If I am feeling particularly theological, I might respond that I am a child of the most high God, and a disciple of his son Jesus. All of these answers are true, and all of them are incomplete. To really know who I am you have to know my story. We know others through their stories, and in fact, we understand who we are through the stories that we tell about ourselves.

When we hear a story that engages us, we enter into it. It enters into our hearts and minds in a way that mere information does not. In his book, *You Are What You Love*, James K.A. Smith argues that more than being a bundle of thoughts and beliefs, humans are, "first and foremost lovers."[1] Taking Saint Augustine as a guide, he argues that, "the center of gravity of the human person is located not in the intellect but in the heart…It is my desires that define me. In short, you are what you love."[2] As a story takes root in our heart, we increasingly identify with it and begin to see ourselves in its light.

Just as every person has their own origin story, so too does every group of people. As Christians, oftentimes we think that our story starts with Jesus. That is not wrong, but it is incomplete. Jesus, as our savior, is the glue that connects us into a much larger story. Through Christ, we are brought into the story of what God is doing in the world now, and what he has been doing since the world began. We are no longer passive bystanders, but we are actors in the grand drama of reality. 1 Peter 2:9-10a tells us, "But you are a chosen people, a royal priesthood, a holy nation, God's special possession, that you may declare the praises of him who called you out of darkness into his wonderful light. Once you were not a people, but now you are the people of God." (NIV). We are the people of God. As the people of God, the stories of the people of God in the Bible are now an integral part of our own stories, and we are caught up into the grander story of what God is doing in the world.

If we are to understand who we are as people, and who we are as Christians, we need to understand the story that we are a part of. This was a problem for the people of Israel as they transitioned from being a loose collection of nomadic tribes into a fixed country. Part of the way that they told their story

---

1. James K.A. Smith, You Are What You Love (Grand Rapids, MI: Brazos Press, 2016), 7.
2 Smith, 9.

is through the names of the places in their land and along the way to their land. As they entered Canaan, they named places along the way, and these place names retell the story of who they are, and who they belong to. Over the next several weeks we will study the story of the people of Israel, and we will look at our own stories in light of what God has done. We will watch as they retell their story through the way that they named places in the land, and we will learn how that gets reflected in our own stories.

What does this look like?

At this point you are probably wondering how this will all work! Over the next few weeks we will be digging into the history of Israel as we read it in the Old Testament. Through this study we will look at five different types of places, and through them, five different ways that God shows up in our stories. The first place is a place of encounter—sooner or later we all have some sort of encounter where we finally decide that God is actually *our* God and we are going to be his people. This is the place of encounter. The second place we will look at is a place of Lament. Simply because we are God's people does not mean that everything will always be wonderful—in fact, it is often very hard. Those are places where we need a place of lament. Another type of place we will visit is the place of disobedience and repentance. Sadly, disobedience is part of the story, and has been since the beginning. When we look at the places where we have been disobedient, we find not only that we grieve God, but that God does not give up on us—we are not left hopeless in our disobedience. The fourth location we will look at is the place of remembrance—these are places where we mark that *something* significant happened, and they remind us of who we are, and who we belong to. The final place that we will look at is the place of victory. There are some battles that are simply impossible for us to win if God does not show up. This was as true for the Israelites as it is for us, and we will look at how God shows up in our lives.

Each week consists of a reading plan for the week which will cover the key verse for the week as well as a larger section of context for that verse, reflection questions related to what is read during the week, an opportunity to reflect on your own life with respect to what has been read, and a simple spiritual practice related to the reading. The reading plan is broken up into five days.

The final week of the study you will have the opportunity to tell your story to the group and to design a rule of life for yourself. As you have been reflecting on your own story you will have seen how God has shown up in your story, as well as where you felt close and where you felt far. Looking at where we have been and where we are can give us a sense of where we are going (or at least a sense of where we *want* to be going). A rule of life is simply a plan[3] for spiritual growth. As you have practiced various spiritual practices through the weeks you will likely have found some that are more effective for you than others—adding these into your consistent rhythm of life is a helpful way to orient towards growth.

Tips For Study

This study is an inductive Bible study. All that means is that we will be looking at what the text says, and we will use those observations to understand what it means in its own context, and then apply that to our own lives. You will not need a commentary or a study Bible to successfully navigate this study, although at the end of the study there will be a list of useful resources for further study/learning.

The key to a successful study is to read carefully. If you have the time, it is helpful to read through the entire passage in one

---

3. Or, if like the author, you hate plans, a roadmap for growth.

sitting. This time through, simply allow the story to wash over you . The goal here is to get the big picture before starting to dig deep. For your daily reading, make some notes about what you noticed. What is repeated? What is referencing something else? What is confusing? Who are the main characters? What stands out to *you*? Look for connections within the text. *Everything* starts with good observations. It is important to note that your observations do not have to be profound—simply noticing that the word LORD is repeated a bunch of times in a particular passage tells you something about that passage!

As you go on to answer the reflection questions, try to think about motivations—why did the people in the story do this thing? Why is that important? What does it have to do with me (or us)? While there are some answers to these questions that are better than others, there are very few wrong ways to answer—the point here is that when we come together as a group each week to discuss the passages, we will explore together and discover what God has for us.[4]

Key Passages For the Week

1 Peter 2:9-10. *But you are a chosen people, a royal priesthood, a holy nation, God's special possession, that you may declare the praises of him who called you out of darkness into his wonderful light. Once you were not a people, but now you are the people of God; once you had not received mercy, but now you have received mercy. (NIV)*

Galatians 3:28-29. *There is neither Jew nor Gentile, neither slave nor free, nor is there male and female, for you are all one in Christ Jesus. If you belong to Christ, then you are Abraham's seed, and heirs according to the promise. (NIV)*

---

4. Of course, there are some wrong answers—if the question is, "Why did the Israelites name Ebenezer Ebenezer", the answer 12 is not correct.

Reflection Questions

1. What does it mean to be the people of God?

_____

_____

_____

_____

2. What do you think about the prospect of exploring your story? What is exciting? What is intimidating?

_____

_____

_____

_____

3. What do you hope to get out of this study?

_____

_____

_____

_____

Spiritual Exercise

Since for this week there isn't really any homework, our spiritual practice is one that we will do together. It is called My thoughts vs. God's thoughts. This is an exercise of the rhythm of prayer. If praying is conversation with God, silence is the listening part of prayer. Through silence, we allow uninterrupted time for the Holy Spirit to speak to us. This particular exercise is a group exercise. Essentially, we will spend five minutes of silence together. The first two and a half minutes simply think—whatever you want to think of: you can ponder your day, or wonder why we bother with this. After two and a half minutes we will have a chance to discuss what the experience was like. After that we will enter into another two and a half minutes of silence. This time try to focus your thoughts on God. Enjoy this time with God—it can contain conversation, listening, or just sitting. When the time is up, we will discuss again.[5] The purpose of this practice is to learn how to sit and *listen* to God. He is the great author of our story, and it is worthwhile to listen to what he may have to say about it.

---

5. Diana Shiflett, Spiritual Practices in Community (Downers Grove, IL: InterVarsity Press, 2018), 27-30.

Week 2

Encounter: Bethel

Genesis 35:15. Jacob called the place where God had talked with him Bethel

Each one of us has had an encounter with God at some point. For some of us it may have been a pretty dramatic experience. For others, it may be something more simple—a realization, or an insight, or a conviction that God is real and true. This held true for the people of Israel too. Their existence as a nation was due to the direct encounter of their ancestors with God. This week we will look at the dramatic encounter that Jacob has with God, and how that resulted in the name of the place Bethel. This place name reminded Israel of the dramatic encounter that they (through their ancestor Jacob) had with God, and it marks the beginning of their story as Israel.

When we read the story of Jacob, he is rather a scoundrel! As the younger brother, he is not supposed to get the larger inheritance. He tricks his father into giving him the blessing that he had intended for his brother Esau, and as a result has to run for his life. That is where we pick up the story this week.

This week we will be reading Genesis chapters 27-35 and we will see how Jacob first encounters God, and how he grows in that relationship.

Key Passages For the Week

The key verses this week are Genesis 28:10-22 and Genesis 35:1-15. These describe Jacob's rationale for naming the place of Bethel, Bethel. It is worth noting that the name Bethel is Hebrew for the phrase House of God. This place marks a critical encounter with God in the life of Jacob.

Reading for the week

The wider passages that we will read this week are Genesis 27-35, which recounts all of Jacob's adventures after he leaves his father's house. Here we will see how his relationship with God develops, and how he changes over time. If you have the time, it will be helpful to read all nine chapters in one go before you start.

Day 1: Genesis 27:1 - 28:22

1. Observations:

_____

_____

_____

_____

2. What stands out most about Jacob's character to you?

_____

_____

_____

_____

3. Do you notice anything about God in this passage?

_____

_____

_____

_____

4. Does anything here remind you of your story?
   In what ways?

_____

_____

_____

_____

Day 2: Genesis 29:1 - 31:21

1. Observations:

_____

_____

_____

_____

2. What stands out most about Jacob's character to you?

_____

_____

_____

_____

3. Do you notice anything about God in this passage?

_____

_____

_____

_____

4. Does anything here remind you of your story?
   In what ways?

_____

_____

_____

_____

Tell Me A Story

Day 3: Genesis 31:22 - 32:31

1. Observations:

_____
_____
_____
_____

2. Have you seen any patterns in Jacob's life so far?

_____
_____
_____
_____

3. Do you notice anything about God in this passage?

_____
_____
_____
_____

4. Does anything here remind you of your story?
   In what ways?

_____
_____
_____
_____

Day 4: Genesis 33:1 - 34:31

1. Observations:

_____

_____

_____

_____

2. What connections or parallels between passages have

_____

_____

_____

_____

3. you noticed so far?

_____

_____

_____

_____

4. Do you notice anything about God in this passage?

_____

_____

_____

_____

5. Does anything here remind you of your story?
   In what ways?

_____

_____

_____

_____

Day 5: Genesis 35:1 - 35:28

1. Observations:

_____

_____

_____

_____

2. What, if anything, has changed in Jacob throughout
   this story?

_____

_____

_____

_____

3. What is revealed about God in this passage?

_____

_____

_____

_____

4. Does anything here remind you of your story?
   In what ways?

_____

_____

_____

_____

Reflection Questions

1. Looking back over all of the readings this week, what do you notice happening with Jacob?

_____

_____

_____

_____

2. Where is God in Jacob's story?

_____

_____

_____

_____

3. Where have you encountered God *in your story?*

_____

_____

_____

_____

4. How did you decide that God would be your God?

_____

_____

_____

_____

Spiritual Exercise

We often think that we have to *do* something to be able to merit God loving us. Rest is an antidote to that. Resting reminds us that we are finite and requires that we trust God to take care of us. Rest is also something that, in our busy society, we often get too little of. So this week, take a day and rest. Sleep in or go to bed early. Spend time with loved ones. Enjoy a hobby. Read a good book or watch a movie. The God that we have encountered is a God who is often found in rest. God's goodness towards us is not earned—so take time to enjoy his goodness through rest.

Week 3

Lament: Abel-mizraim

Genesis 50:11. When the Canaanites who lived there saw the mourning at the threshing floor of Atad, they said, "The Egyptians are holding a solemn ceremony of mourning." That is why that place near the Jordan is called Abel Mizraim.

We live in a world that is simultaneously extravagantly magnificent, and deeply broken. When we eat a good meal, or see a beautiful sunset, or spend hours enjoying the company of someone that we love, we get a sense of how amazing the world we live in is. We experience the opposite of that as well, though. We experience pain and sickness. Loved ones die and relationships are broken. We have all experienced places where we just *hurt*. Sometimes we think that because we are Christians, we will somehow become immune to the brokenness and suffering that are in the world. The sad truth is that we are not. The good news is that God does not abandon us to our suffering and, in fact, enters into it with us. The Israelites too experienced this. This week we will look at a short story of lament, as well as a couple of psalms that help us to understand lament.

Shortly after Jacob died, Joseph and his brothers returned to Canaan to bury him. They came with a large entourage, and their lament was so grievous that the people of the land named the place *Abel-mizraim* or Mourning of the Egyptians. At this point, God's promises to Israel were coming true—the people of Israel had begun to be a blessing to the nations through Joseph, and they were no longer a small tribe of shepherds. The fact that they were recipients of the promises of God did not exclude them from suffering however, and that is what we will see here.

In addition to looking at the story of how Joseph and his brothers mourned and had good cause for lament, we will take a look at two psalms. One of the amazing things about the psalms is that they are so honest—in them we find glorious praises to God, and we also find deep laments. God has generously provided us with words for all the range of emotions that we can feel—anger, joy, hope, and deep pain. The psalms of lament help us to process our pain and actually hold on to God in the middle of it.

Key Passages For the Week

The key verses this week are Genesis 49:29-50:14. In this short passage we see Jacob giving his sons instructions for his funeral, his death, and the way that his sons mourn for him. It is interesting to see how this grief is so clear that even the people around note it.

Reading for the week

Our reading this week is a bit scattered. In addition to our key verses, we will look at Genesis chapters 12 and 28, which reiterate the promises that God made to the Israelites, Genesis 47:13-50:14, which shows us how God fulfilled his promises, and Psalms 22 and 69, which give us words for our deep pain.

Day 1: Genesis 12:1–9, Genesis 28:10–15

1. Observations:

_____

_____

_____

_____

2. How do these passages parallel each other?

_____

_____

_____

_____

3. Do you notice anything about God in this passage?

_____

_____

_____

_____

4. Does anything here remind you of your story?
   In what ways?

_____

_____

_____

_____

Day 2: Genesis 47:13–48:22

1. Observations:

_____

_____

_____

_____

2. Do the events in these passages reflect the promises from yesterday's passages? If so, how?

_____

_____

_____

_____

3. Do you notice anything about God in this passage?

_____

_____

_____

_____

4. Does anything here remind you of your story? In what ways?

_____

_____

_____

_____

Day 3: Genesis 49:1–50:14

1. Observations:

_____

_____

_____

_____

2. What do you notice about lament in this passage?

_____

_____

_____

_____

3. Do you notice anything about God in this passage?

_____

_____

_____

_____

4. Does anything here remind you of your story?
   In what ways?

_____

_____

_____

_____

Day 4: Psalm 22

1. Observations:

_____

_____

_____

_____

2. What is striking about this passage?
   Is there anything surprising?

_____

_____

_____

_____

3. Do you notice anything about God in this passage?

_____

_____

_____

_____

4. Does anything here remind you of your story?
   In what ways?

_____

_____

_____

_____

Day 5: Psalm 69

1. Observations:

_____
_____
_____
_____

2. Is there anything new to you in this passage?

_____
_____
_____
_____

3. What is revealed about God in this passage?

_____
_____
_____
_____

4. Does anything here remind you of your story?
   In what ways?

_____
_____
_____
_____

Reflection Questions

1. Looking back over all of the readings this week, what strikes you most about lament?

_____

_____

_____

_____

2. Where is God in the midst of the lament that we have looked at?

_____

_____

_____

_____

3. What has caused lament *in your story*?

_____

_____

_____

_____

4. Have you seen or felt or noticed God in the midst of lament?

_____

_____

_____

_____

Spiritual Exercise

The practice for this week is service. This can be done either individually or as a group, but the task here is to serve someone. This can be as simple as doing something unexpected for a friend or family member. It may seem strange to tie service to lament. What we find, however, is that service is often a wonderful response to other people's lament—when we are in our worst moments, we often do not want advice, but having a brother or sister sit with us and help carry the burden can be deeply helpful. Use this opportunity to serve someone in and unexpected and loving way (just doing your chores does not count)

Week 4

Disobedience & Repentance: Taberah & Kibroth-hattaavah

Numbers 11:1-3. Now the people complained about their hardships in the hearing of the LORD, and when he heard them his anger was aroused. Then fire from the LORD burned among them and consumed some of the outskirts of the camp. When the people cried out to Moses, he prayed to the LORD and the fire died down. So that place was called Taberah, because fire from the LORD had burned among them.

It is an unfortunate fact that human beings sin. As the apostle Paul writes in Romans 3:23, "all have sinned and fall short of the glory of God." There is no person on earth who has escaped that. We have all seen the destruction that sin causes and often it is that destruction that drives us to repentance. This week we will be reading a story of two places where the people of Israel were disobedient to God and the disastrous results of that disobedience. We will also see how God remains faithful in the midst of our disobedience.

Key Passages For the Week

Our key passages this week are Numbers 11:1-3 and Numbers 11:33. Both of the places mentioned in these verses are named because of the disastrous consequences of the Israelites rebellion. They are an immediate reminder of Romans 3:23a, "The wages of sin is death."

Reading for the week

Our larger passage for the week is Numbers 11:1-12:16. These passages show the way that the Isrealites rebelled against God, and how God responded to their rebellion. They also show how God responded to their repentance, as well as how God provided for them. As you read this week it is helpful to contrast the complaints of the Israelites with the laments that you looked at last week in the psalms. Through the psalms we see that we *do* have permission to complain to God and to even be angry with him. There is a kind of complaint and anger that engages with God, and there is a kind of complaining and anger that wants nothing to do with God.

Day 1: Numbers 11:1–15

1. Observations:

_____

_____

_____

_____

2. What is going on in this passage?
   Why might God be so angry?

_____

_____

_____

_____

3. Do you notice anything about God in this passage?

_____

_____

_____

_____

4. Does anything here remind you of your story?
   In what ways?

_____

_____

_____

_____

Day 2: Numbers 11:17-35

1. Observations:

_____

_____

_____

_____

2. What parallels do you notice between this passage
   and yesterdays?

_____

_____

_____

_____

3. Do you notice anything about God in this passage?

_____

_____

_____

_____

4. Does anything here remind you of your story?
   In what ways?

_____

_____

_____

_____

Day 3: Numbers 12:1-16

1. Observations:

_____

_____

_____

_____

2. What parallels do you notice between this passage
   and yesterdays?

_____

_____

_____

_____

3. Do you notice anything about God in this passage?

_____

_____

_____

_____

4. Does anything here remind you of your story?
   In what ways?

_____

_____

_____

_____

Day 4: Psalm 142

1. Observations:

_____

_____

_____

_____

2. How does this differ from the complaints we saw earlier?

_____

_____

_____

_____

3. Do you notice anything about God in this passage?

_____

_____

_____

_____

4. Does anything here remind you of your story?
   In what ways?

_____

_____

_____

_____

Day 5: Numbers 11:1-12:16

1. Observations:

_____

_____

_____

_____

2. Do you notice anything new reading through this time?

_____

_____

_____

_____

3. What is revealed about God in this passage?

_____

_____

_____

_____

4. Does anything here remind you of your story?
   In what ways?

_____

_____

_____

_____

Reflection Questions

1. As you look at the readings this week what strikes you about the gravity of sin?

_____
_____
_____
_____

2. Where do you see God offering grace in the midst of disobedience?

_____
_____
_____
_____

3. Where have you been disobedient?

_____
_____
_____
_____

4. Where has God restored you?

_____
_____
_____
_____

Spiritual Practice

This week our practice is self-examination and confession . This is a hard rhythm to add to our lives—we are rarely inclined to admit (even to ourselves) that we are not always the wonderful person that we think we are. We all sin and we all need to turn from those sins and ask forgiveness. The key to our practice this week comes in Psalm 139:23-24 where the psalmist writes, "Search me, O God, and know my heart; test me and know my thoughts. See if there is any wicked way in me, and lead me in the way everlasting." The point of our self-examination is not to make ourselves feel wretched, rather it is "to surrender my weaknesses and faults to the forgiving love of Christ and intentionally desire and embrace practices that lead to transformation." Read over Psalm 139:23-24 and make it your prayer. As you pray, take time to look back at your day. Where have you felt God's presence? Where have you felt his absence? Where have you actively rebelled against him? Bring those areas specifically to God and ask for forgiveness and for power not to sin again. Are there areas where you need accountability? Seek out someone to help you with those areas.

Week 5

Remembrance: The Altar of Witness

Joshua 22:34. And the Reubenites and the Gadites gave the altar this name: A Witness Between Us—that the LORD is God.

So far we have looked at places where God has met Israel, where Israel has lamented, and where Israel has disobeyed and repented. These experiences are universal and they shape who we are. This week we get to look at places of remembrance. As Israel entered into the promised land, they found themselves divided—the tribes of Reuben, Gad, and the half-tribe of Manasseh inherited their land on the eastern side of the Jordan river. When they returned to their lands they built an altar as a witness that they too belonged to the people of Israel. They needed to ensure that they would remember who they were, and that the rest of Israel would remember who they were.

Key Passages For the Week

Our key passages this week are Joshua 22:10-12, 24-28, and 34. These passages describe how the tribes that inherited land on the eastern side of the Jordan river set up locations of memory to remind them and the rest of Israel who they were.

Reading for the week

Our larger passages for the week are Numbers 32, Deuteronomy 3:1-20, and Joshua 21:42-22:34. These passages show how the lands east of the Jordan were promised to the Reubenites, Gadites, and Manassehites, and how they were faithful in carrying out their promises. They also tell of the construction of the Altar of Witness.

Day 1: Numbers 32:1-42

1. Observations:

_____

_____

_____

_____

2. What is going on in this passage?

_____

_____

_____

_____

3. Do you notice anything about God in this passage?

_____

_____

_____

_____

4. Does anything here remind you of your story?
   In what ways?

_____

_____

_____

_____

Day 2: Deuteronomy 3:1-20

1. Observations:

_____

_____

_____

_____

2. What parallels do you notice between this passage
   and yesterdays?

_____

_____

_____

_____

3. Do you notice anything about God in this passage?

_____

_____

_____

_____

4. Does anything here remind you of your story?
   In what ways?

_____

_____

_____

_____

Day 3: Joshua 21:43-22:8

1. Observations:

_____

_____

_____

_____

2. How does this passage refer to the previous passages you
   have read?

_____

_____

_____

_____

3. Do you notice anything about God in this passage?

_____

_____

_____

_____

4. Does anything here remind you of your story?
   In what ways?

_____

_____

_____

_____

Day 4: Joshua 22:9-27

1. Observations:

_____

_____

_____

_____

2. What is happening in this passage?
   Does this remind you of any previous readings?

_____

_____

_____

_____

3. Do you notice anything about God in this passage?

_____

_____

_____

_____

4. Does anything here remind you of your story?
   In what ways?

_____

_____

_____

_____

Day 5: Joshua 22:28-34

1. Observations:

_____

_____

_____

_____

2. What is the altar a reminder of?
   Why is that important?

_____

_____

_____

_____

3. What is revealed about God in this passage?

_____

_____

_____

_____

4. Does anything here remind you of your story?
   In what ways?

_____

_____

_____

_____

Reflection Questions

1. Why was it important to the Reubenites, Gadites, and Manassehites to have a reminder?

   _____

   _____

   _____

   _____

2. What is the purpose of memory in this story?

   _____

   _____

   _____

   _____

3. What reminds you of who you are?

   _____

   _____

   _____

   _____

4. Why is it important to be reminded of who you are?

   _____

   _____

   _____

   _____

Spiritual Practice

This week we have two practices, both of which are related to celebration. The first practice is individual. Make a list of everything that you are grateful for and spend at least 5 minutes every day thanking God for it. Try to add to your list every day this week. There is nothing too trivial or too extravagant. This practice helps us to remember the real source of everything in our life, and to practice gratitude for it. The next practice is corporate. This week we will take communion together as a group.

Communion is not magic. It does not do anything to us. But it is important. It is a reminder to us of what Jesus has done. It reminds us that he has forgiven us and that we have been given the power to follow him faithfully. Through his strength, we get to imitate him and start to look like him.

When we take the juice and take the bread, they go into our body, and we digest them. The elements of them are used to give us energy and to build our bodies. In the same way, Christ's spirit is living inside us, empowering, and building us up in his image. Jesus is as close to you as this bread and juice that you will eat. He is our life, our fuel, and he is constantly present in us. Communion lets us act out that reality in a way that we can see, taste, and feel.

Week 6

Victory: Ebenezer

1 Samuel 7:12. Then Samuel took a stone and set it up between Mizpah and Shen. He named it Ebenezer, saying, "Thus far the LORD has helped us."

There are times in our lives where we are in way over our heads. We find ourselves in a situation where we simply cannot get out of it on our own. What happens to us then? Israel found themselves in such a situation. They had lost the Ark of the Covenant (through their own foolishness) and had been oppressed by the Philistines. They had been treating God as though he was a tool to be used, not a God to be served and loved. This week we will see what happened when they finally returned to him wholeheartedly, and we will see how he rescued them.

Key Passages For the Week

Our key passage this week is 1 Samuel 7:3-14. This passage recounds how Israel returned to God, and how he helped them by liberating them from Philistine oppression. The place where God rescues them is named Ebenezer, which means "stone of help."

Reading for the week

Our larger passages for the week are 1 Samuel 4:1 - 7:17. These passages show how Israel lost the Ark of the Covenant, how it was returned, and how they eventually returned to God.

Day 1: 1 Samuel 4:1-22

1. Observations:

_____

_____

_____

_____

2. What is going on in this passage?

_____

_____

_____

_____

3. Do you notice anything about God in this passage?

_____

_____

_____

_____

4. Does anything here remind you of your story?
   In what ways?

_____

_____

_____

_____

Day 2: 1 Samuel 5:1-12

1. Observations:

_____
_____
_____
_____

2. What is happening with the Ark and the gods of the
   Philistines?

_____
_____
_____
_____

3. Do you notice anything about God in this passage?

_____
_____
_____
_____

4. Does anything here remind you of your story?
   In what ways?

_____
_____
_____
_____

Day 3: 1 Samuel 6:1-12

1. Observations:

_____

_____

_____

_____

2. How does this passage refer to the previous passages you
   have read?

_____

_____

_____

_____

3. Do you notice anything about God in this passage?

_____

_____

_____

_____

4. Does anything here remind you of your story?
   In what ways?

_____

_____

_____

_____

Tell Me A Story

Day 4: 1 Samuel 6:13-7:2

1. Observations:

_____

_____

_____

_____

2. What is happening in this passage?

_____

_____

_____

_____

3. Do you notice anything about God in this passage?

_____

_____

_____

_____

4. Does anything here remind you of your story?
   In what ways?

_____

_____

_____

_____

Day 5: 1 Samuel 7:2-17

1. Observations:

_____
_____
_____
_____

2. Why is it important that the place be named Ebenezer?
   Are there any other Ebenezer's in this story?

_____
_____
_____
_____

3. What is revealed about God in this passage?

_____
_____
_____
_____

4. Does anything here remind you of your story?
   In what ways?

_____
_____
_____
_____

Reflection Questions

1. What do you think of there being two places named Ebenezer?

   _____

   _____

   _____

   _____

2. What might it matter for the Israelites to know that God was with them up to a certain point?

   _____

   _____

   _____

   _____

3. What is an Ebenezer—"God came this far with me" in your life?

   _____

   _____

   _____

   _____

4. Why is it significant to you to remember that place?

   _____

   _____

   _____

   _____

Spiritual Practice

Our spiritual practice for this week is worship. Spend at least ten minutes in worship every day this week. We have a God who has showed up for us, and he deserves our worship. Take an expansive view of worship. There is much more to worship than merely singing (although singing and making a joyful noise to God is a wonderful way to worship him). Try some ways of worship that you are not used to. For instance, you could read a psalm every day, or write a poem. You could take with a friend or neighbor about how God has been good to you. Perhaps you could try dancing with joy or cry out in lament. Or even just sit in silence before him for a while listening. Any of these can be a way of expressing your worship to him. The important part is to make it a point to spend at least ten minutes daily in worship.

Week 7

A Story and a Plan

Psalm 107:1-3. Give thanks to the LORD, for he is good; his love endures forever. Let the redeemed of the LORD tell their story—those he redeemed from the hand of the foe, those he gathered from the lands, from east and west, from north and south.

For the last 5 weeks we have been looking at the stories of how Israel became Israel through the places that they named. Each of these place names reflects some particular aspect of their story as a people. Just like them we have places and events in our lives that reflect how God has uniquely shaped us and how we have walked in or out of relationship with him. Some of these events have been painful. Some of them we probably regret. Each one of them has formed a part of who we are today. As we have looked at our lives, we have seen where God has worked and where we have grown. This week we will be looking at our own stories, and looking at how we can join God in writing the next chapters.

The first task of this week is to write out your story so that you can tell it. It is important to actually write the story out, simply because when we have written the story we have a clearer idea of what we want to say. It also serves as a marker for us of where God has been and what he has done.

The next task for this week is to design a rule of life. Simply put, a rule of life is a plan or a roadmap of practices that you will put in place in your life to help you to grow. It is very important when thinking of a rule of life to remember that this *is not* a way of gaining favor with God or of earning merit. Rather a rule of life is just a recognition that growth takes practice and it is planning to practice for growth.

Writing Your Story

For most of us the idea of writing out our life story is pretty daunting. This does not have to be the case, however. To begin with, take a look at all of the ways that you have reflected upon your story in the last few weeks. Try to put them into order chronologically and see where and how they connect. Creating a timeline can be very helpful here—note the key events and when they happened. Take note of the people who were critical to your growth along the line. Take your time with this—even though we have been looking at our stories the last five weeks, putting everything in order can take time. You might need to take a break or you may find that going through everything in one take works best for you.

As you put together your story, the following questions may be helpful to you:

1. How do these events connect?
2. What are the high points?
3. What are the low points?
4. What patterns do I see?
5. Where is God in my story?

When you have completed your story, take some time to look back on it. Look at where you were, and where you are now. See where you have grown and where you have struggled. It can be easy to undervalue our own story, but the reality is that we are "fearfully and wonderfully made" (Psalm 139:14a). Looking at your story will help you as you look at the next step for this week, designing a rule of life.

Writing a Rule of Life

A rule of life is simply a set of practices that you put into place to help to orient yourself towards growth. Adele Ahlberg Calhoun describes it as, "unique and regular rhythms that free and open each person to the will and presence of Christ. The spiritual practices of a rule provide a way to partner with the Holy Spirit for personal transformation."[6] Throughout this study you have experienced a few different spiritual practices. If you have participated in Rooted, you also participated in the 7 Rooted Rhythms: Daily Devotion, Prayer, Freedom from Strongholds, Service, Generosity, Celebration, and Sharing your Story. These are all spiritual practices. A rule for life is a way of planning to fit those practices into your life.

When planning a rule of life, I have found it helpful to break things down into 5 to 10 minute rhythms, hour long, daily, weekly, monthly, and yearly. A 5 to 10 minute rhythm is something that you can practice at any time—it only takes 5 to 10 minutes and is easily started or stopped. Start with these. Hourly take more work—perhaps you wish to pray for an hour—in that case you will need to plan time for that specifically. By breaking practices up into daily, weekly, monthly, and yearly it becomes more likely that we will actually do them—we have time to plan and set aside for more complicated activities. Do not be alarmed by the idea of yearly practices! Start small and where you are—it is much more important to our growth to take small healthy steps every day than a few grand gestures every once in a while.

---

6. Adele Ahlberg Calhoun, Spiritual Disciplines Handbook (Downers Grove, IL: InterVarsity Press, 2015), 31.

A Sample Life Timeline

This is a sample timeline that may be helpful in giving you ideas on how to go about writing your story. This is only one way to put together a story—if this feels artificial or difficult, feel free to do something else.

- Born—Oldest of the family
- Elementary school—nothing too notable
- VBS—accept Jesus as savior—an encounter moment
- Grandma dies—a moment of lament
- Junior High—another moment of lament
- Wandering away from God—time of rebellion
- Mission trip—an encounter with God and repentance
- Aimlessness but seeing God's faithfulness
- Graduate college—a victory
- The present—studying the Bible and committed…

It can be helpful to the process of telling your story (and to the process of understanding your story) if you put the timeline into something like a chart. The timeline above might look something like this as a chart:

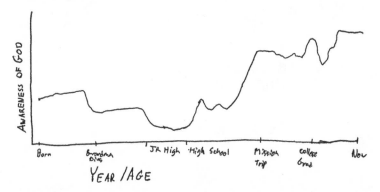

Be as creative as you wish in your storytelling and your story explaining—this is your story, and you can tell it better than anyone else!

A Sample Rule of Life

This is a rule of life designed with the concept of rhythms as described above.

Daily Rhythms:

- 5 minutes praying every morning
- Read at least 3 paragraphs of the Bible
- Practice listening prayer for 3 minutes every night

Weekly Rhythms:

- Life Group
- Attend Church

Monthly Rhythms:

- Serve at church
- Spend a day with the family doing something fun
- Read a good book

Yearly Rhythms:

- Vacation
- Read the Bible
- Revise Rule of Life

Resources

This section offers a few resources that may be helpful to you as you continue your walk with Jesus.

Celebration of Discipline by Richard Foster

If you are interested in learning more about the spiritual disciplines, the book *Celebration of Discipline* by Richard Foster is an excellent introduction. This book has been foundational for many as they encounter the spiritual disciplines. Foster's thesis is that, "The desperate need today is not for a greater number of intelligent people, or gifted people, but for deep people," and that the disciplines are a gateway into that depth. He categorizes the disciplines into three general groupings, Inward, Outward, and Corporate disciplines. He then proceeds to describe the various subspecies of discipline within those larger categories. Foster does an excellent job of taking a topic that is often unfamiliar and perhaps even frightening and providing both a rationale for the practice, and practical examples of how the practice works. In a similar way, he does an excellent job of pointing out how while the disciplines are activities, they are not at all a form of works righteousness.

Spiritual Disciplines Handbook by Adele Ahlberg Calhoun

For most of us the idea of spiritual disciplines is a bit nebulous. The book *Spiritual Disciplines Handbook* offers a helpful introduction to a multitude of different practices. Where the strength of *Celebration of Discipline* is in its explanation of the why of the disciplines, *Spiritual Disciplines Handbook* offers the how. In this book Adele Ahlberg Calhoun offers over seventy-five discrete disciplines with a one-page overview, followed by a short explanation of why and how you might incorporate this discipline into your life. This book is particularly helpful when designing a rule of life, but it is also just a friendly guide if you are stuck in a spiritual rut and want to try something different. Each of the disciplines is explained in a way that is easy to follow, and is minimally intimidating. Some of the example practices found in our study were based upon these disciplines or combinations of them.

The Good and Beautiful God by James Bryan Smith

The Good and Beautiful God once again introduces us to the spiritual disciplines. This is an excellent book to study together with a group as it walks through the false narratives that we often have about who God is and how we are to relate with him. He breaks down how we have often misunderstood the Good News, and then explains how the Gospel is actually much better and more beautiful than we may have realized. If you only read one book from this list, this is the book to read. Each chapter is capped by a small spiritual training exercise for the week to help put the learning from the week into practice. His writing is winsome and accessible and this book is highly recommended.

Facilitator's Guide

Week 1. What's your Story?

This week is primarily about explaining what we are doing, why we are doing it, and getting ready for the group. So a couple of points that are critical to discuss:

1. Emphasize confidentiality—people will not be willing to share their story if it is not safe. We want this to be a safe place. In the event that things come up that are difficult, please reach out the church—we have resources available

2. We will be reading the stories of the people of Israel and trying to understand why they named places what they named them. These places are markers of critical moments in their history and are important to understanding who they are as the people of God. In the same way, we experience moments like these and they are critical to understanding ourselves as God's people

3. Let people know up front that we will be sharing our longer stories at the end of this series. This will be a time for us to affirm each other and to see how God is at work in us and in each other.

4. The reflection questions in the study materials are a great place to start discussion each week as you talk about the passages that you have read. Let your group members know that they should come ready to discuss these questions each week.

Discussion this week

Our key texts for the week are:

1 Peter 2:9-10. But you are a chosen people, a royal priesthood, a holy nation, God's special possession, that you may declare the praises of him who called you out of darkness into his wonderful light. Once you were not a people, but now you are the people of God; once you had not received mercy, but now you have received mercy. (NIV)

Galatians 3:28-29. There is neither Jew nor Gentile, neither slave nor free, nor is there male and female, for you are all one in Christ Jesus. If you belong to Christ, then you are Abraham's seed, and heirs according to the promise. (NIV)

Both of these passages deal with our identity as the people of God. Since we are God's people, the stories of God's people in the Bible are directly relevant to us—even though the Israelites are not our biological ancestors (at least for most of us), they are our spiritual ancestors and their story matters.

General Timeline

Each week will be slightly different, but this timeline is provided to give you a rough framework for discussion times. The timeline provided here assumes a 90 minute meeting. Feel free to adjust it according to the needs of your group and even the needs of the week—some weeks are likely to take longer than others.

- General hang out time, icebreaker, announcements, etc... (10m)
- Pray to start the evening (5m)
- Read the key passage/passages together (5-10m)
- Discuss the reflection questions.
- Where is God in this story? (20m)
- Where is God in our stories? (30m)
- Pray together (15-25m)
- Plan next week (1-10m)

Week 2. Encounter—Bethel

This week we will be looking at Jacob's life. In particular we will be looking at how Jacob came to have God as *his* God, rather than being the God of his father and grandfather. The chapters that we will be reading cover most of Jacob's life—starting with when he gets the blessing that his father had intended for his brother Esau, and continuing until after he reconciles with his brother, and commits himself to God.

Discussion this week

The key verses this week are Genesis 28:10-22 and Genesis 35:1-15. These describe Jacob's rationale for naming the place of Bethel, Bethel. It is worth noting that the name Bethel is Hebrew for the phrase House of God. This place marks a critical encounter with God in the life of Jacob.

As you discuss the passages this week, keep an eye on Jacob's trajectory. He truly starts out as rather a scoundrel—not the sort of person that most of us would pick as a spiritual leader! He is serially dishonest, and so are many other members of his family—his mother, his wife, and his father-in-law all exhibit this pattern. Another important thing to note is how God renames Jacob to Israel. In the ancient near east, names were very important so what might we be learning about Jacob through this name change?

A couple of possibly helpful details that are not obvious from the text—the name Jacob in Hebrew sounds a lot like the word for heel—Jacob is named as a heel right from the start, and his name reflects that. The name Israel means "struggles with God."

Discuss the reflection questions as a group. As always, try to reflect on each person's story in light of the story for this week. Ask followup questions about where people encountered God. It is entirely possible that there are those in your group who have not completely decided that God will be their God. That is ok—one thing that we see with Jacob's trajectory is that he starts out pretty equivocal in his commitment to God.

Week 3. Lament – Abel-mizraim

This week we will be looking at a place of lament. Lament is one of those things that we often don't understand very well as Christians. When Paul tells us in Philippians 4:10, "Rejoice in the Lord always. I will say it again: Rejoice," we have a tendency to think that means we cannot be sad. The reality is that in our lives trouble will come, and we have to acknowledge that! The place that we are looking at is a place where Joseph and his brothers went to bury his father and to mourn for him.

Discussion this week

The key verses this week are Genesis 49:29-50:14. In this short passage we see Jacob giving his sons instructions for his funeral, his death, and the way that his sons mourn for him. It is interesting to see how this grief is so clear that even the people around note it. The other passages that we will read are Psalms 22 and 69, which are psalms of lament.

As you discuss the passages this week, keep an eye on how God has fulfilled the promises that he gave to Jacob—being blessed by God and being part of his family does not exempt them from suffering.

Psalm 22 is the famous psalm that Jesus quotes on the cross. But before Jesus spoke it, David wrote it to express *his* deep pain. Keep an eye on the trajectory in Psalm 22. David begins by expressing his deep pain and confusion. Around the middle, however, he switches to confidence that God will indeed help him. Psalm 69 is similar. David describes his pain and pours out his feelings to God (including some pretty unpleasant ones where he wishes that God would pay back the harm caused to him). Keep in mind how the exit from the pain is by going through it.

Discuss the reflection questions as a group. As always, try to reflect on each person's story in light of the story for this week. What has been lamented in your group? Allow people to sit with that—we do not have to tell people that everything is ok when everything is not ok. One thing that the psalms show us is that *honestly* telling God how we feel and giving *all* of the pain to him lets us move forward.

Week 4. Disobedience & Repentance—Taberah & Kibroth-hattaavah

This week we have the difficult topic of disobedience and repentance. These are probably the least pleasant aspects of our Christian life—we do not like to admit to the fact that we are still in the process of being made like Jesus. We do fail and there are consequences for those sins and failures. While there are consequences, there is also grace. God remains faithful to us even when we are unfaithful to him.

Discussion this week

Our key passages this week are Numbers 11:1-3 and Numbers 11:33. Both of the places mentioned in these verses are named because of the disastrous consequences of the Israelites rebellion. They are an immediate reminder of Romans 3:23a, "The wages of sin is death."

These passages are kind of shocking—plague and death seem like kind of drastic responses to grumbling and complaining. As you discuss this with the group keep an eye out for God's mercy in the midst of the punishment. Notice that the complaining is a longing to return to Egypt (Numbers 11:4)—this is coming from people who have *seen* God's presence in their midst to provide, protect, and guide, and they still want to return to slavery!

Discuss the reflection questions as a group. As always, try to reflect on each person's story in light of the story for this week. Areas of disobedience can be scary to share—DO NOT FORCE anyone to share and/or break into same gendered groups to discuss if that feels more comfortable. It is important to remind people of God's grace and faithfulness, not merely his justice and righteousness. God is always righteous and merciful, just and faithful.

Week 5. Remembrance – The Altar of Witness

There are times in our lives when we need to be reminded of who we are. This week we will be talking about a place that reminds Israel of its identity. In the same way, there are places in our lives that remind us of who we are.

Discussion this week

Our key passages this week are Joshua 22:10-12, 24-28, and 34. These passages describe how the tribes that inherited land on the eastern side of the Jordan river set up locations of memory to remind them and the rest of Israel who they were.

As you discuss the passages for the week, take note of why it might be important for the tribes east of the Jordan to be reminded of who they are. Why might it be important for those west of the Jordan to remember that as well?

Discuss the reflection questions as a group. As always, try to reflect on each person's story in light of the story for this week. This week, focus on where are those places/what are those things that remind the group of who they are? These are *deeply* important parts of our identity, so it is important to remember them rightly.

Communion

This week you will also be taking communion as a group. It is *very* important to note that communion is not some magical thing that happens when we drink wine/juice and eat bread together. Traditionally the Friends have avoided taking communion with the elements because communion with Christ is something that is available to us continuously. This is very true. But it is also true that we humans are powerfully affected by symbols, and the symbolism of communion is no different. Communion does not make us more saved or more holy. It does serve as tangible act that reminds us that Christ's Holy Spirit lives inside of us to empower us and build us up. While it may not be a common activity, it is easy to do communion together and the reminder that it provides can be powerful for us. If you have never taken communion together as a group, here is one way that you can go through it together

What you'll need

Juice (or wine, water, soda, something to drink) and Bread (or crackers, etc…)

Process

The process is simple. Discuss what communion is. There are some sample words below, but you don't need to use these specifically. Reading a scripture about communion is a good idea—we get what we know about communion from the scriptures, so we should always return to them!

Communion is not magic. It doesn't do anything to us. But it is important. It is a reminder to us of what Jesus has done. It reminds us that he has forgiven us and that we have been given the power to follow him faithfully. Through his strength, we get to imitate him and start to look like him.

When we take this juice and take this bread, they go into our body, and we digest them. The elements of them are used to give us energy and to build our bodies. In the same way, Christ's spirit is living inside us, empowering and building us up in his image. Jesus is as close to you as this bread and juice that you will eat. He is our life, our fuel, and he is constantly present in us. Communion lets us act out that reality in a way that we can see, taste, and feel.

Read a scripture describing communion:

> ²³ *For I received from the Lord what I also handed on to you, that the Lord Jesus on the night when he was betrayed took a loaf of bread,* ²⁴ *and when he had given thanks, he broke it and said, "This is my body that is for you. Do this in remembrance of me."* ²⁵ *In the same way he took the cup also, after supper, saying, "This cup is the new covenant in my blood. Do this, as often as you drink it, in remembrance of me."* ²⁶ *For as often as you eat this bread and drink the cup, you proclaim the Lord's death until he comes.*
>
> *1 Corinthians 11:23-27*

Leader breaks the bread and serves it to the person on their right

This is Christ's body, broken for you.

Leader passes the cup to the person on their right

This is Christ's blood, shed for you.

The person next to of you serves to their right … until all have been served.

When all have been served, eat together.

Pray together to close your time.

Week 6. Victory—Ebenezer

Some situations are just impossible. This week we will be looking at a place where the Israelites were stuck and only God could save them. God came through and they won a great victory against unlikely odds. We get to explore how Israel returned to God, and how that provoked a reaction from the peoples around, and how God ultimately rescued them.

Discussion this week

Our key passage this week is 1 Samuel 7:3-14. This passage recounds how Israel returned to God, and how he helped them by liberating them from Philistine oppression. The place where God rescues them is named Ebenezer, which means "stone of help." Our larger passages for the week are 1 Samuel 4:1 - 7:17. These passages show how Israel lost the Ark of the Covenant, how it was returned, and how they eventually returned to God.

As you discuss the passages this week take note of the time gap between the return of the Ark and Israel returning to God. Why might it provoke their neighbors when they do fully return to the Lord? It is also interesting to note that a place called Ebenezer is mentioned twice in the passages this week. We do not know for certain if these two places are exactly the same location, or if they are different places. It is significant that they both mark *very* different ways of interacting with God.

Discuss the reflection questions as a group. As always, try to reflect on each person's story in light of the story for this week. This week, focus on where are those places/what are those things that remind the group of ways that God has given them victory. Remembering where God has rescued us and given us a victory helps us to trust that he can do it again.

Next week is going to be somewhat different. Be sure to remind your group that next week is storytelling week, as well as their chance to design a rule of life for themselves. Pick an order/ask people to sign up for their turn to tell their story. It may be useful to plan on a couple of weeks for storytelling to ensure that everyone gets enough time to tell their story. Plan on at least twenty minutes per person for storytelling, as well as a few minutes for questions and prayer after each story.

Week 7. A Story and a Plan

Congratulations! You have made it through to the end! This week we get to tell our stories to the group. This makes the week a little bit different than the previous weeks. Plan on allocating at least twenty minutes for each person to tell their story (have space for longer if needed, though). Most importantly, *you* need to be ready to tell *your* story! If you need to, split this week into multiple weeks, just to ensure that everyone has an opportunity to speak. Remind your group once again of the importance of confidentiality. Our stories are personal and need to be treated as special and valuable. Do not share outside without permission (unless the person is actively harming or going to harm others—in that case there may be a need to contact someone!)

Flow for this week

Unless there is a person in your group who has already expressed interest in telling their story, it is helpful if you tell yours first to break the ice. Take notes on the stories that you hear—look for how God has been at work in people's lives! Be aware of the patterns in people's lives—how God has shown up, how they have interacted with others, etc…

Be sure to let the storyteller tell their story without interruptions. Once the story has been told, the group can ask questions and/or offer affirmations to them. Thank the storyteller for sharing, and ask if anyone has noticed how God has worked in the person's life. The purpose of comments and questions here is to help the storyteller see that God is involved in their life, especially in any ways that they might have missed.

Conclude each story with a time of prayer for the storyteller. Pray a blessing over them and invite the rest of the group to pray for them as well.

A sample timeline for a single story would be:

1. Tell the story (20-30 min)
2. Questions and answers (5 min)
3. Prayer (5-10 min)

Notes

Calhoun, Adele Ahlberg. Spiritual Disciplines Handbook. Downers Grove, IL: InterVarsity Press, 2015.

Smith, James K.A. You Are What You Love. Grand Rapids, MI: Brazos Press, 2016.

CPSIA information can be obtained
at www.ICGtesting.com
Printed in the USA
LVHW030702170522
718962LV00001B/141